SUFFOLK COAST
FROM THE AIR 2

SUFFOLK COAST
FROM THE AIR 2

PHOTOGRAPHS MIKE PAGE TEXT PAULINE YOUNG

HALSGROVE

First published in Great Britain in 2009

British Library Cataloguing-in-Publication Data
A CIP record for this title is available from the British Library

ISBN 978 1 84114 973 8

HALSGROVE
Halsgrove House,
Ryelands Industrial Estate,
Bagley Road, Wellington, Somerset TA21 9PZ
Tel: 01823 653777   Fax: 01823 216796
email: sales@halsgrove.com

Part of the Halsgrove group of companies
Information on all Halsgrove titles is available at: www.halsgrove.com

Printed and bound by Grafiche Flaminia, Italy

FOREWORD

In this sequel *Suffolk Coast from the Air 2* Mike Page has sought to record some of the changes to the coastline since his original 'Suffolk Coast from the Air' was published in 2006. Some pictures make worrying viewing. We wonder what will remain of the coastline in a century's time if sea incursion is allowed to continue at its present rate. Government policy dictates what will remain for our grandchildren's children to enjoy. Aerial photography is an excellent way of recording change and, additionally, these pictures intensify our awareness of the beauty and often the remoteness of much of the Suffolk coastline.

James Hoseason OBE

ACKNOWLEDGEMENTS

We are indebted to the following for their expert help.

Richard Adderson, Peter Boggis, Dr Jenny Lawrence, Judy Speed
and Mike's co-pilots Peter Day, Tim Ball, Brian Barr, and Jonathan Howes.

Mike Page, Strumpshaw
Pauline Young, Norwich, 2009

DEDICATION

For Gillian Page and John Young

*The Danes, the Dutch and the French have all in their time harassed communities down this strip of land
but none has ever done as much damage as the sea.*

From *Suffolk* by John Burke 1971

BIBLIOGRAPHY

Burke John, *Suffolk*, Batsford 1971
Buxbaum Tim, *Suffolk*, Shire Publications 1996
Dymond David & Northeast Peter, *A History of Suffolk*, Phillimore 1995
Edwards Russell, *The Suffolk Coast*, Terence Dalton 1991
Higgins David, *The Beachmen*, Terence Dalton 1987
Jebb Miles, *Suffolk*, Pimlico 1995
Malster Robert, *Saved from the Sea*, Terence Dalton 1974
Palmer Terry, *The Suffolk Coast*, Heritage House 1976

Pevsner Nikolaus, *The Buildings of England - Suffolk*, Penguin 1975
Phelps Humphrey, *Lowestoft to Southwold - old photographs*, Alan Sutton 1994
Scarfe Norman, *The Suffolk Landscape*, Alastair Press 1987
Scarfe Norman, *The Suffolk Guide*, Alastair Press 1982
Vesey Barbara, *The Hidden Places of East Anglia*, Travel Publishing 2003
Williamson Tom, *East Anglia*, Collins 2006
Wren Wilfred, *Ports of the Eastern Counties*, Terence Dalton 1976

INTRODUCTION

Since our first *Suffolk Coast from the Air* was published in 2006 there have been significant changes to the landscape and these are recorded here in this book. Most striking among the changes is the rapid rate of erosion of vulnerable areas particularly around Easton Bavents, Covehithe and Benacre and also the southward drift of the shingle bank on Orford Ness. Elsewhere along the coast attempts to provide protection by beach reclamation and the addition of substantial rock groynes have been noted. With future changes such as the building of Sizewell 3 its site has been pictured so that there will be a 'before and after' record. Where there has been little change, an attempt has been made to provide different snippets of information to those in the first book. We hope you will enjoy every page.

Mike Page
Pauline Young
2009

Mike Page's cameras are a Canon 1D Mk2 digital with a 80-200 2.8 lens and a Canon 1D Mk 3 digital with a 24-105 L lens. His high wing Cessna 150 is ideal for the job, he photographs from an open window, his camera is hand-held to counter vibration or turbulence. Always he is accompanied by a safety pilot who flies the aircraft when Mike is taking pictures and for the rest of the flight helps to keep a good lookout.

All royalties from the sale of this book, as with all our others, will go to charity

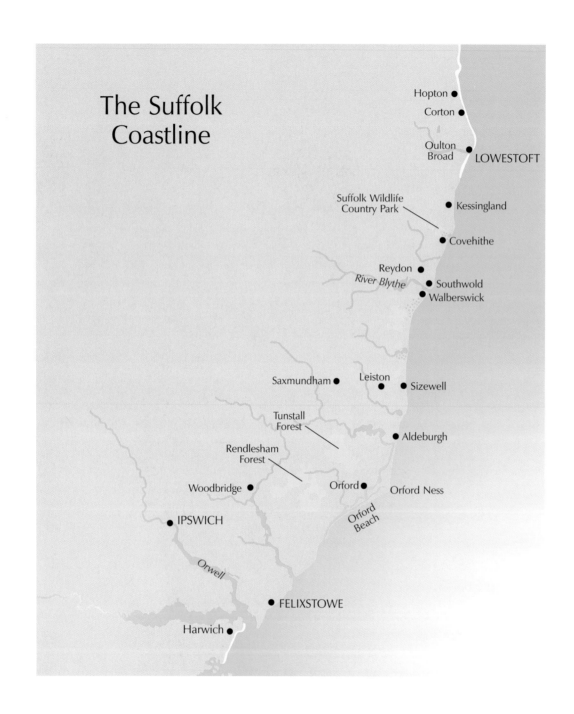

The Suffolk Coastline

Hopton ●

Corton ●

Oulton
Broad ●
LOWESTOFT

Suffolk Wildlife
Country Park —— ● Kessingland

● Covehithe

Reydon ●
River Blythe
● Southwold
● Walberswick

Saxmundham ●   Leiston
● Sizewell

Tunstall
Forest

● Aldeburgh

Rendlesham
Forest

Woodbridge ●   Orford ●   Orford Ness

● IPSWICH   Orford
Beach

Orwell

● FELIXSTOWE

Harwich ●

Cattawade Creek

Cattawade Creek flows into the River Stour (pron. 'Stoor') and hence into Harwich harbour. The newer bridge in the foreground carries the main London–Norwich railway line. Daniel Defoe in his *Tour through the Eastern Counties of England* (1724) sent his servants and baggage on horseback across the bridge and along muddy tracks to Ipswich whilst he took the more scenic route by boat along the Stour and up the Orwell.

Brantham

Brantham is more significant in industrial history than are most Suffolk villages for it was here that Xylonite (an early form of cellulose) was developed. The factory had moved out from Hackney to farm buildings in Brantham. With the introduction of this new material, lives of tortoises whose shells had been sacrificed for combs and elephants whose tusks were used for piano keys were spared.

Railway triangle at Manningtree

Flying overhead Essex Mike Page took this intriguing picture of a triangle of railway lines. The London–Norwich line crosses Middlebridge Creek and runs south to north. The line bottom left heading east to Harwich was opened in 1854 and extended in 1882 to accommodate the growth of Parkeston Quay with its steamer traffic. The east to north curve ran between Harwich and The Midlands thereby avoiding London, today the line carries goods traffic and has a few local services.

Overhead Manningtree looking towards Suffolk

Opposite: **New Mill Creek at Stutton**
Only the name is a reminder that once there was a succession of tidal mills on this site, the last was demolished in 1908.

The Royal Hospital School and Alton Water

The Tattingstone Valley immediately north of Stutton in 1978 was sacrificed to provide Ipswich with additional water. It was pumped four miles from the River Gipping to fill the four-hundred-acre reservoir. The Royal Hospital School was set up to educate the sons of seafarers but now is open both to boys and girls. Established 1712 at Greenwich it moved out to Holbrook in 1933. The land on which it is built was a gift to the Admiralty from a tea merchant in gratitude because none of his cargo ships was lost during the First World War.

Holbrook village

The church contains the tomb of Judge John Clench, one of the judges in the trial of Margaret Clitherow (1586). She was accused of harbouring Catholic priests in her York home. She refused to testify to avoid implication and subsequent torture of her children. The standard punishment for refusal to plead was death by crushing. Her last words apparently and incredibly were *"God be thanked I am not worthy of so good a death"*.

Holbrook has the rare distinction of being the last place in England where people died of the plague, as recently as 1918. The virus was thought to have been carried in the holds of sailing barges.

Holbrook Creek

Brick rubble for road-making at the Royal Hospital School was brought in by barge along Holbrook Creek.

Shotley village

Separate from the hamlet of Shotley Gate which lies on the Point itself, both villages are a distance from Shotley Church whose main feature seems to be the absence of a steeple. A naval cemetery is contained within the churchyard and buried there are many navy personnel including boys from HMS *Ganges* and German sailors who died during the First World War. An old sailors rhyme runs:

'Shotley church without a steeple
Drunken parson, wicked people"

Shotley Gate

From here there are superb views along the River Orwell to Levington and Landguard Point and across the Stour estuary to Harwich. Offshore one of the most bloodthirsty battles in English history was fought and ever after this strategic piece of land has been called Bloody Point. The crews of sixteen Viking ships were murdered by King Alfred's troops AD885. Not one but two Martello Towers were built on this promontory demonstrating its strategic importance during the Napoleonic Wars.

Shotley Gate Marina

Site of HMS *Ganges*

Only the famous mast and some empty buildings remain of what was once a Naval Training Station for boys wanting to enter the Royal Navy. Established in 1899 HMS *Ganges*, a three-decker training ship, was moored in the River Stour. The base later moved onshore to Shotley Point where the harsh regime lasted until it closed in 1976. The traditional mast manning ceremony involved young sailors climbing the one-hundred-and-forty-three-foot mast with one boy standing on the top button which measured only eleven inches across. Whereupon they all saluted.

Ipswich

A river link to the North Sea has ensured the town's prosperity over the centuries. Much of the town centre has been redeveloped in the last fifty years.

The end of navigation on the River Orwell

Upstream the Orwell is joined by the River Gipping. Centre picture stands the home ground of Ipswich Town's football club in Portman Road. The name Portman originated in the Middle Ages. The Port Men were paid in kind rather than in cash, they were given grazing rights on a piece of land which became known as the Portman's Marshes part of which became Portman Road.

Neptune Marina

Modern housing and mooring for leisure cruising has become a feature of several cities fortunate enough to have rivers running through their centres. Neptune Marina was opened in 2000 in the Wet Dock and has a two-hundred-and-fifty berth capacity.

The dock entrance to Ipswich Marina

The Wet Dock's handling facilities demonstrate Ipswich's continuing importance as a port. Seven hundred years ago Dunwich, before Dunwich's demise, was a rival to Ipswich in importance as a port.

Belstead Brook enters the Orwell

Ipswich Docks

Within the dock complex there's a Container Terminal at Cliff Quay and a RoRo facility. Barley and fertiliser are two of the main exports whilst coal, timber, phosphates and petrol are brought in. In the sixteenth century wool was exported in huge quantities.

The Orwell Bridge
Completed in 1982 the bridge provides part of the essential commercial route between London, The Midlands and the Container Terminal at Felixstowe. It serves also as a bypass round the southern side of Ipswich.

25

Woolverstone Marina

The quiet little village developed new life by providing mooring for two hundred craft and is the base for the Royal Harwich Yacht Club. There was a bit of excitement in the village's earlier life. Cat House in whose window a model cat now sits was part of a smuggling enterprise two centuries ago. A white stuffed cat would be placed in the window when customs officials were not around. Catastrophe if cat got it wrong!

Heading out to the North Sea

Levington

This compact village with its distinctive red brick church tower (1636) is best known perhaps for its Levington Composts, developed here by Fisons after they discovered that the local crag had value as a fertiliser. Arthur Ransome took a fancy to the Orwell Estuary and lived in this village whilst writing the children's story *We Didn't Mean To Go To Sea*. His boat *Peter Duck* was built on the opposite bank at Pin Mill where he kept his seven-ton cutter *Nancy Blackett*.

Suffolk Yacht Harbour

Sailing barges used to work along the now dried up Levington Creek which is a few hundred yards upriver. The yacht harbour was first operational in 1967. The large red vessel, now used as a clubhouse, was once a lightship moored off Cromer.

Trimley Marshes

In 1990 the Suffolk Wildlife Trust were able to lease Trimley Marshes from the port of Felixstowe to mitigate the loss of Fagbury Marshes which went for port expansion. Most of the species found here in the wet grazing, reedbeds and lagoons have colonised since the acquisition. Wading birds and wildfowl can be watched from a series of hides.

The Port of Felixstowe
From modest beginnings as the Felixstowe Railway and Pier Company in 1875 and weathering extreme damage during the 1953 floods, the complex has developed to become the largest container port in the UK.

High tech operations...

...and not so high tech!
Two cranes were damaged when a ship broke free from its moorings during a gale on March 2008. Ironically the ship was carrying new dockside cranes for Felixstowe!

Colourful containers

Harwich Haven

From Norman times Harwich (Essex) has played a vital role defending trade routes, a role entirely out of proportion to its size. Sometimes known as Orwell Haven, in Roman times it was a refuge and guarded by Walton Fort, now rubble on the sea bed. This is the finest natural harbour between the Thames and the Humber and has no need of constant dredging to keep the port open at all states of the tide. Harwich has been the departure point for packet boats to Holland for four centuries and today the port, part of which is the Parkeston Quay complex (top of picture) has many roles including docking for cruise liners and a handling facility for cargo containers. Harwich is one of the few remaining places where Trinity House, responsible for the maintenance of navigational aids such as lighthouses and buoys, has a presence.

Trinity House vessels at Harwich

The confluence of the Rivers Stour and Orwell meeting at Shotley point and flowing together in Harwich Harbour.

Felixstowe looking north
Industry and the seafront give way to houses and marshes and the mouth of the River Deben.

Beyond the estuary, the town and the River Deben, lies the shingle of Orford Ness and on the horizon Sizewell Nuclear Power Station.

Landguard Point

A fort at Landguard Point has been guarding the land - and more significantly the approach from the sea - since the reign of Henry VIII. During the Anglo-Dutch wars of 1667 the enemy realised that until Landguard Fort was put out of action a landing on the beach was impossible so an attempt was made to scale the fortress. It failed miserably. In the middle distance a ferry has just left Parkeston Quay heading probably for Holland, proving the two countries resolved their difficulties.

Landguard Fort

The present fort, there have been two previous ones, dates from 1745. The semicircular shape was created in 1872 to provide improved barracks. The fort was armed with heavy guns during both World Wars. Today the only captives are migratory birds attracted by the bright lights of the docks. Unsuspectingly they fly into vertical nets put there by an Ornithology Group who ring and record the birds then send them on their way.

Landguard Common

Sixty-four acres of land between the fort and the sea have been recognised as an SSSI and since 1979 have been a Nature Reserve. Rare plants of the shingle are found here including sea kale and sea holly and there's a colony of nesting terns. The white mast is part of the port radar system.

Beach reclamation

The aim of the Southern Felixstowe Coastal Strategy is to enhance the frontage and provide protection from flooding for the town for the next 150 years. Extra sand has been added to the beach and the old wooden groynes have been replaced by substantial rock groynes. The Martello Tower stands on Wireless Green which in the First World War was the site of a telegraphy station communicating with destroyers patrolling the North Sea.

Looking west across to Harwich and Shotley Point

Felixstowe

The town's heyday was when it became fashionable as a seaside resort. This was thanks in part to the advent of the railway and to the pleasure steamers which called in at the pier en route to London or Great Yarmouth. The Empress of Germany enjoyed her stay in 1891, which is rather more than Mrs Wallis Simpson did in 1936 when for six weeks, with two friends and their maids, the party waited for Mrs S's divorce to be made absolute so that she could marry King Edward VIII. She complained that the house in which they stayed (now demolished) was too cramped.

Cobbolds Point

Named after a member of the Ipswich brewing family whose house was here, Cobbolds Point is particularly vulnerable to erosion, hence the fishtail groynes. The Martello Tower at the mouth of the Deben is one of a chain of nine between Felixstowe and Aldeburgh.

Opposite: **Beach Huts**

The beach hut developed from the bathing machine where one had privacy to change into a swimming costume and, unlike the beach hut, was on wheels to allow the occupant to be trundled into the sea thereby avoiding an unseemly display of naked flesh. The beach hut is akin to the garden shed both in construction and in that its many devotees add individual and enthusiastic homely touches to make it their own. It's doubtful if Mrs Simpson would have enjoyed a beach hut.

Oh I do like to be beside the seaside!
Beach huts, summerhouse and the garden shed.

Felixstowe Ferry

The foot ferry across to Bawdsey gave the hamlet its name.

The wayward currents and shifting sandbank demonstrate how challenging the sail up to Woodbridge can be!

Felixstowe Ferry

Boat building and boat repairs, a couple of pubs, a café and a church - that's about it at Felixstowe Ferry.

Thames Barge *Pudge*

Now owned by the Thames Barge Sailing Trust the 67-ton *Pudge* was built at Rochester in 1922. Thames Barges were designed to carry cargo up and down the east coast and coastal rivers. There are similarities with the traditional Norfolk wherry, both were designed for local trade although wherries rarely went out to sea. Both were owned and operated by men who didn't have money to spare and kept their craft in good but economical order. The single black wherry sail was coated with soot, tar and fish oil to preserve it, the Thames Barge's three red sails were treated with red ochre, mixed with fish oil and horse urine. Both must have been particularly aromatic after their annual treatment! A couple of dozen Thames Barges remain and they make a wonderful sight when racing at various east coasts venues such as Pin Mill during the summer. Here *Pudge* is seen in the shallow waters of the River Deben.

Waldringfield

For thirty years around the turn of the nineteenth century the tranquillity of this lovely village was spoiled by a cement works, although the populace was doubtless grateful to have jobs there. Mud from the bed of the River Deben was mixed with chalk brought in by barge and baked in kilns to produce the cement which was then reloaded into barges for transporting. With the invention of the rotary kiln, one of which was installed at Claydon near Ipswich, the Waldringfield cement works became redundant and the village regained its peace and quiet.

Woodbridge
The famous Woodbridge Tide Mill is left of picture, the mill pool is now part of the Marina. Many are of the opinion that Woodbridge is the most attractive small town in Suffolk.

Opposite: **Realising assets**
In 1862 Waldringfield church was derelict. The vicar found a novel way to raise funds for its restoration. Coprolite is fossilised dung and this was dug out from the church glebe lands. Up to twenty-five barges a week carried away the coprolite from the village quay. Today's nice little earners are mooring fees, maybe!

Woodbridge Tide Mill

Built in 1793 this is the last tide mill in England whose machinery is capable still of grinding corn which it does on Demonstration Days. It's worked by the incoming tide filling the mill pool. The water is held behind a sluice gate as the tide recedes. The pressure of water within the pool keeps the sluices shut then water is diverted through the race to turn the wheel after the tide goes out. It can work two hours either side of high tide and during that period can grind 4cwt of flour. It last worked commercially in 1957. The Woodbridge Tide Mill Trust restored the mill and opens it to the public.

Overhead Waldringfield looking downriver to the sea
The River Deben is no longer a waterway for commercial traffic and because of breaches in the sea wall the areas of salt marsh have expanded over recent years.

Ramsholt Quay
A ferry across to Kirton Creek Brickworks ran in the 1950s. The bricks were transported downriver by barge.

Bawdsey Ferry aka Felixstowe Ferry

The Bawdsey Peninsula
Shingle continues to move southwards and here is building across the mouth of the Deben.

Bawdsey looking west

Bawdsey Manor (left of picture), acquired by the Air Ministry in 1936, can be considered the birthplace of radar. Here Sir Robert Watson-Watt and his colleagues developed an experimental coastal warning system having begun their work at Orford Ness.

THV *Patricia 3* off Bawdsey

Patricia 3 has been the flagship of the Trinity House Lightship Service since 1982. She patrols the waters of the British Isles enabling the crew to inspect floating buoys and light vessels, refuel lighthouses and mark ship-wrecks where they're likely to cause a hazard to navigation. And if you fancy a sea cruise it's possible to book a seven-day passage, there's room on board for twelve passengers.

Bawdsey: The destructive power of the sea
A First World War gun emplacement falls.

Martello Tower at Bawdsey East Lane Point

No Government funding here!

New rock defences completed in June 2009 will now protect this vulnerable part of the coastline from the sea, for many years to come.

Funding for the £2.5 million scheme was raised by a ground-breaking community project set up by the East Lane Point Trust. Blocks of land in adjacent villages were sold off for house building to raise funds for the new sea defences.

Bawdsey: East Lane Point

New sea defence works were taking place at the time this picture was taken. The sea has claimed several Martello Towers along this coastline. Whilst by the time the towers were built all risk of French invasion had gone, they have served useful purposes subsequently as coastguard lookouts, gun sites and holiday homes. The lagoons were man-made to store water for irrigation, with the clay from the construction used to bolster the sea walls.

Bawdsey Village

Alderton

An eighteenth century Alderton rector sent his gardener every Saturday with a bowl of soup to the poor... but only if they had been in church the previous Sunday. The church tower fell into the nave and the nave was repaired in 1864 but the tower is absent. The Suffolk Heritage Coastal Path starts here and continues all the way to Lowestoft scarcely ever having to touch a road.

Hollesley ('Hoselee') village

There have been several settlements here. First came Iron Age man (750BC–AD40). He developed the use of primitive agricultural tools made of metal, thereby paving the way for more efficient ways of producing food. In 1886 a Colonial College and Training Farm was created for boys wishing to make a new life farming in the colonies. From 1906 a training establishment was set up for the unemployed and from 1939 the site has been a Youth Detention Centre.

Shingle Street looking south

The whole area is a bird watcher's paradise

Opposite:
Shingle Street
This is one of the most remote places on the Suffolk coast. There's no main village, just a cluster of houses, some coastguard cottages and a pub which was a victim of wartime bombing. A Wellington bomber aiming for the Martello Tower, missed and bombed The Lifeboat pub instead. The shingle continues to build as it is washed southwards.

Havergate Island

This RSPB reserve and the one at Minsmere were the first places in England where avocets returned to breed in 1947. The avocet is the logo of the RSPB. It's possible to visit the Island by boat from Orford Quay but only by prior arrangement with the RSPB. Spoonbills, sandwich and common terns and blackheaded gulls all have colonised here. The mouth of the Butley River is abeam the southernmost tip of the island.

Opposite: **The mouth of the River Ore**

It's difficult now to imagine how barges worked up river to Butley, Orford and Snape. The river's name changes to the Alde just below Aldeburgh.

The lighthouse

There has been a lighthouse on Orford Ness since 1634, this is the third. The first two were in turn swept away by the sea. The lighthouse shares with The Ness at Lowestoft the distinction of being the most easterly point in Britain although Lowestoft keeps very quiet about that! The black tower in the background was put there by the Royal Aircraft Establishment in 1928 as an experimental rotating loop beacon. Today it serves as a viewing area.

Opposite: **Orford Ness**

This is one of the 'secret', i.e. 'official secret', places of Britain. In 1928 a hush-hush experimental navigation beacon was installed here together with early work on radar. 'Pagodas' were constructed during the Cold War period of the 1960s testing triggers for nuclear warheads. The pagodas' construction was such that following an explosion their roofs would fall inwards thereby containing the contaminated material within the buildings. The 'Cobra Mist' era of the 1970s saw early-warning device work being undertaken, the sixty feet high masts are now re used for transmissions by the BBC World Service, among others. In fact quite a lot has been going on here over the years one way or another. But different sorts of goings on were common in earlier centuries, Customs men used to hide in the shingle in wait for smugglers. Orford Ness can be reached by boat across the Ore from Orford Quay.

Orford Ness, Havergate Island and Orford

The shingle bank, The King's Marshes and the pools are all part of Orford Ness with 'Stony Ditch' running through the middle. The shingle runs all the way north to Aldeburgh. Havergate Island has in the past been inhabited, as late as just before the Second World War the Brinkley family grazed sheep and cattle here. During the war the island was used for target practice, a shell destroyed a sluice flooding part of it so making it ideal for the return of the avocet in 1947. The RSPB bought the island in 1948. The shingle is building southwards all the time so the mouth of the River Ore (joined by the Butley River or Creek) is becoming further and further away from the open sea.

Orford

Orford was once a port exporting wool and importing wine but eventually the town was cut off from the sea by the encroaching shingle. During the reign of Edward III, Orford provided the King with ships at the Siege of Calais. The 90-foot high keep, the only remaining part of Orford Castle, was begun in 1165 and was close to the sea when it was built. The church stands prominently in the middle of the town. It was in the church that the first ever performance (1958 as part of the Aldeburgh Music Festival) of Benjamin Britten's 'Noye's Fludde' was performed. The town is renowned for the sale of Butley Oysters. Historically it was a Rotten Borough sending to Parliament two members with a population so small that this could not be justified. Sir Robert Walpole, the country's first Prime Minister, chose the title Earl of Orford when elevated to the House of Lords (1742). Rather strange because he had no connection whatsoever with Orford.

Orford Castle

All that remains of the castle is the polygonal keep whose walls are 10 feet thick and is considered to be the finest Norman keep in Britain. Castles, or parts of them as here at Orford, are the most enduring symbols of the Norman Conquest. It has a commanding position over what would have been an important harbour. Built of septaria, a local stone akin both in composition and location to flint, it's a mass of limestone pebbles or ovoid stones filled with calcite and found in chalk deposits. At one time septaria was thought to be dinosaur droppings! The keep, an early landmark for shipping, survived moves to demolish it in the eighteenth century and now is maintained by English Heritage.

Orford Quay

Even with the shingle build-up the port continued to operate, bringing cargoes in and out along the River Ore. But eventually Aldeburgh stole the trade. Today the only maritime activity is a sight-seeing trip along the river or to the RSPB's Havergate Island. The National Trust operates a ferry across to Orford Ness on which there's a five-mile hiking trail and a guided tour of the Ness which includes a visit to the pagodas.

The jetty on Orford Ness

Towards Aldeburgh

The long shingle spit south of the mouth of the River Ore is building southwards all the time. It widens considerably on Orford Ness then narrows towards Aldeburgh. This area has been called 'Suffolk's wilderness'. When the spit reaches Slaughden (where Aldeburgh begins today) it's so narrow that the sea could break through at any time. Slaughden built ships and was a fishing port but the last traces of the village were washed away in a violent storm a mere hundred years ago. The river, which mysteriously changes its name from the Ore to the Alde downriver takes a sharp turn westwards towards Snape.

Slaughden

The Martello tower is the last in a line which stretches from the South Coast. Its quatrefoil shape is unusual, most are circular or ovoid. It was the only survivor of the storm which washed away the remains of Slaughden. The Landmark Trust rents it out for holidays.

Opposite: **Martello Tower**

There were one hundred and five towers built between Seaford in Sussex and Slaughden, most often referred to as Aldeburgh. Some have been demolished, some have fallen into the sea but many remain as a reminder of the perceived threat posed by the Napoleonic Wars. Afterwards several were occupied by the coastguard in the battle against smuggling. The moat which once surrounded the tower has been washed away on the seaward side.

Aldeburgh

What we see now is only half a town. The houses facing the beach, including the mediaeval Moot Hall, were once in the town centre before the rest of the town was washed away by the sea! The prominence of Thorpeness, 'ness' (Fr)= nose, and Sizewell Nuclear Power Station are northwards, whilst abeam Sizewell to the west is the town of Leiston.

Aldeburgh

The church with its fourteenth-century tower contains a memorial to poet George Crabbe whose poem 'Peter Grimes' was the inspiration for Benjamin Britten's opera. Benjamin Britten is buried in the churchyard. On the beach is Maggi Hambling's large sculpture of two broken scallop shells with the Crabbe/Britten quotation "I hear those voices which will not be drowned". The 3.7m high steel sculpture has aroused much local controversy. It has stood since 2003 on the shingle at the north end of the town and is a memorial to Benjamin Britten who walked on the beach there. Another memorial to the great composer is in the church, a stained glass window by John Piper depicting three of Britten's works.

Snape

The River Alde is navigable and tidal as far as Snape bridge. The Aldeburgh Music Festival came to Snape Maltings in 1947 and has become its annual focus. The Maltings have become a centre for the arts. There was occupation here by the Anglo-Saxons. A burial longship much like the one at Sutton Hoo near Woodbridge was discovered in 1862, and there was a priory here until the Dissolution. Across the river on the lonely Iken promontory stands a church, derelict since a thatch fire in the 1960s. Sailing schooners worked up to the coal yards here two hundred years ago. Aldeburgh stands on the horizon.

Aldeburgh and the River Alde looking towards Snape

Aldeburgh looking south
At some point the River Alde assumes the name of the River Ore but no one is certain exactly where!

Thorpeness

Thorpeness has a make-believe fairytale quality about it. It was here in 1910 that railway magnate Stuart Ogilvy began the creation of a whimsical village, elsewhere described as a 'seaside garden suburb' and sometimes 'part of an eccentric film set'. It centres round the mere, a shallow sixty-five acre pleasure lake with islands where children to this day can enjoy boating in relative safety. The hand dug lake was inspired by Ogilvy's friend J M Barrie and Barrie's story of *Peter Pan*. Two water towers are disguised; houses are built in styles of previous periods, the village has an atmosphere unlike anywhere else.

The House in the Clouds

Possibly the best known building in Thorpeness, this is a disguised former water tower (the other water storage tank was in what looked like a Tudor Gatehouse - see below). Until 1940 the water used to be pumped seemingly from under the windmill (a former post mill - now a Visitor Centre). The corn grinding mill was imported from neighbouring Aldringham. The water was stored at the top of the house and accommodation was on the lower levels but now the whole house has been converted to provide holiday accommodation. In a forward-looking move the church (built 1936) is dedicated rather than consecrated so is available for any faiths.

Thorpeness

Centre picture is the two-storey 'Tudor' gatehouse where once water tanks were concealed.

The Ness

Gradually the Ness has been building up with eroded materials washed down from Dunwich, but the dynamics of this coastline are complicated and material is on the move constantly. There used to be a Beach Company based here. The Beach Companies (forerunners of the lifeboat service), whose stated aims were the rescue of shipwrecked mariners and the salvage of their ships, made their money from salvage operations and often are reported to have turned out to sea only after salvage agreements had been made!

Sizewell Power Stations A and B looking north towards Minsmere and Lowestoft Ness

Sizewell (from Sisa's well) was a small fishing village before 1961 when the Nuclear Power Station was commissioned. Sizewell A was brought on line in 1966 and fed power into the National Grid. It was a first generation Magnox reactor, now obsolete and has been decommissioned. There have been concerns about the safety of nuclear power stations and regular monitoring takes place. On two occasions there have been countrywide elevated radiation levels - the first was 1976-77 when the Chinese were testing their nuclear weapons and the second was in 1986 at the time of the Russian Chernobyl disaster. So it would seem that fears of radiation from Sizewell and the other British Nuclear Power Stations are groundless.

Sizewell B

This is a single pressurised water reactor built 1987-95 and is expected to have a commercial viability at least until 2035.

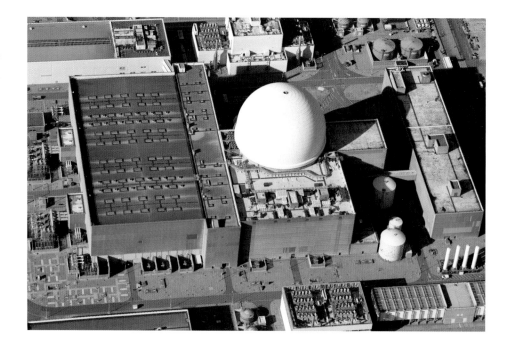

Sizewell B and C sites

Agreement was reached in 2008 to build another nuclear power plant which should be on line by the 2020s.

Minsmere

The coast path from Sizewell to Dunwich passes Minsmere. In 1940 the Minsmere levels, which had been drained for grazing a hundred years previously, were flooded again to hamper possible enemy invasion and the area was declared a prohibited zone. Towards the end of the war four pairs of avocets, attracted by the deserted land, returned to breed. In 1947 the RSPB negotiated the lease and opened the Minsmere Nature Reserve two years later. As the land dried out the avocets took off for wetter conditions at Havergate Island but the conditions were favourable to the marsh harrier which now breeds at Minsmere.

RSPB Minsmere

Forty years ago the RSPB constructed shallow lagoons and scrapes close to the sea wall on the site of the former Minsmere Broad. With a change to wetter conditions in part of the site the avocets returned. The scrapes attracted terns (little, common and sandwich), the ringed plover, and oystercatchers together with over two hundred other species living in different areas of the reserve over the year. In 1976 the RSPB bought the site which has become a birdwatchers' mecca.

Autumn at Minsmere

Minsmere Sluice Looking North

Dunwich Heath

The area is part of the Suffolk Sandlings where the sandy soil is poor and acidic. Pine, gorse and heather flourish as in this July picture. Centre picture are the former Coastguard Cottages converted to holiday accommodation, the Tea Shop and Information Centre, all operated by the National Trust.

Dunwich Sculpture

Three 20 foot high sculptures of waves, collectively entitled 'Storm Surge', have been erected temporarily (2008) on the clifftop at Dunwich. The National Trust Warden says that they were commissioned to highlight the plight of the eroding coastline.

A peaceful clifftop holiday

Dunwich early one March morning

Dingle Marshes November 2007

Dingle Marshes next to Dunwich village and the adjacent Westwood Marshes together have Britain's largest uninterrupted area of freshwater reedbeds. Reed for thatching is an important commercial crop and freshwater reed is preferred. Parts of the marshes are drained to provide summer grazing but this November picture shows how vulnerable they are to sea surges. Dunwich is the town described as having been 'drowned by the sea' and certainly so much has eroded that there's very little left of what was once a thriving port. But the demise of Dunwich was caused also by the silting up of the harbour and the forcing of the river mouth further and further northwards so cutting off all possibilities of trade.

What's been going on here?
Your guess is as good as ours!

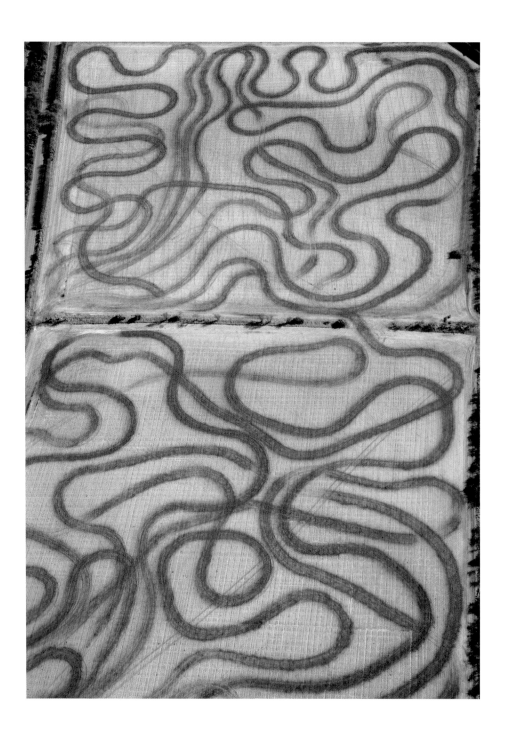

**Dingle Marshes Sea Breach
November 2006**

**Dingle Marshes Sea Breach
November 2007**

Opposite: **Dingle Marshes May 2008**
In the distance are Walberswick, the River Blyth and Southwold.

Westwood, Dingle and Corporation Marshes and the Dunwich River

Walberswick

A favourite Suffolk holiday destination, this small village becomes crowded on summer weekends. In the Middle Ages Walberswick was a shipbuilding port which handled timber, coal, grain, fish and salt. In the fifteenth century it had thirteen ships trading with Iceland, with the duty paid going to the churchwardens. In the wetland is the course of the old Dunwich River.

The River Blyth

The course of the river has changed considerably over the centuries and originally, because of a spit across what is now the harbour mouth, flowed along the coast and reached the sea at Dunwich Haven. In 1328 the sea breached the spit and from then on the Blyth flowed directly into the sea here at Walberswick. An artificial cut was made in 1590 to form the present harbour. In the 1750s the river was made navigable up to Halesworth. Keels, then later wherries, picked up a cargo from sea-going ships tied up in Southwold harbour. The success of the enterprise depended upon the river and harbour mouth being kept free of silt and when this failed the trade dwindled to nothing. Today only pleasure craft have sufficient draught to enter the harbour and the River Blyth is no longer navigable past Southwold.

Southwold to the right, Walberswick to the left with extensive flooding to its marshes November 2007

Walberswick: Tinker's marshes January 2008

SOS

The Walberswick Sea Defence Group are here assembled (17.2.2007) into an SOS message which mirrors that formed by the inhabitants of Happisburgh in Norfolk whose clifftop village is crumbling into the sea. There are no cliffs at Walberswick but there *is* low lying land and the village is under threat both from the sea and the river. The message to the authorities is the same as Happisburgh's: "Do something to save our village from invasion by the sea".

Walberswick, the River Blyth and Southwold

From the air Walberswick church looks enormous but it's a church built within a church or rather within church foundations. When Henry VIII dissolved the monasteries the church lost its income from tithes so the parishioners could no longer afford the upkeep of such a large church building. First the bell was sold then the congregation dwindled as a series of fires over two centuries destroyed most of the village. By 1749 there were only one hundred residents and they lived in twenty houses. Much of the old church was sold as building material although the tower was left intact and a new nave was built from the old one. Recycling is nothing new.

The Blyth Estuary

The Blyth Navigation (the navigable river) opened in 1761 and ran between Southwold and Halesworth, its main cargo was coal shipped in from the north of England. But by 1884 it had run into financial trouble. It was used infrequently until 1910 and was abandoned in 1934. Much of the trouble was the vast amount of labour and expense it took to keep the waterway dredged. It was said that at low tide a horse and cart could be driven across the river from Walberswick to Southwold. At Blythburgh the estuary is now flooded permanently because of a break in the sea wall.

Blythburgh church - the cathedral of the marshes

There are more than 500 mediaeval churches in Suffolk and Blythburgh's is among the best, but its magnificence hasn't always been appreciated. After the spire collapsed (and wasn't replaced) in the mid sixteenth century the building suffered both neglect and vandalism. Fallen angels (the wooden sort) from the magnificent roof, were dumped in a pile in the churchyard. Then along came Oliver Cromwell's men who stabled their horses in the nave, took pot shots at the remaining angels (the shot holes are still there) and fired bullets into the church doors. A hundred years later ravens started nesting in the rafters and they were pot shotted too. It took William Morris's Society for the Protection of Ancient Buildings to put matters right, which to their credit they did without their usual Victorian enthusiasm and therefore much earlier work remains including the painted ceiling. A local puritan had already destroyed the coloured glass windows, the replacement plain glass gives the whole a light and airy feeling. The pew ends have carvings of the Seven Deadly Sins. Hypocrisy is praying with his eyes open, Pride is wearing fine clothes, Slander's mouth is open showing a slit tongue and Greed has a distended stomach.

Blythburgh

The church stands in a prominent position on higher ground overlooking the estuary. Sadly the busy A12 bisects the village.

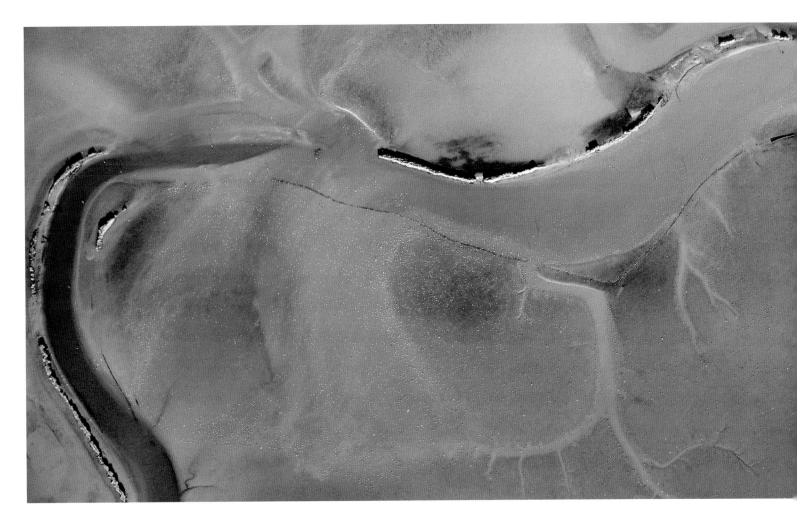

Blyth Mudflats

Southwold harbour entrance
The protection at the northern side of the harbour entrance is new (for the previous installation see next picture).

Southwold

Southwold is a compact town but even so there are several greens which were deliberately created for firebreaks following a disastrous fire in 1659 which destroyed most of the buildings.

Southwold

Work started on the harbour in 1906. An old photograph shows a wooden-hulled fishing smack, an iron-hulled steam drifter and a Thames Barge all tied up alongside the Harbour Inn.

Southwold Seafront

Here are the famous beach huts which, allegedly, change hands for the price of a modest house in some other parts of the country. The tall chimney belongs to the equally famous Adnams Brewery who, amidst great local sadness, have recently abandoned their custom of making local deliveries by dray horse.

Opposite: **The lighthouse, built well inland because Southwold has suffered its share of cliff erosion, has been here since 1890.**

St Edmund's church, Southwold

Like Blythburgh's this is one of the most magnificent of the mediaeval Suffolk churches. But it was almost a piece of serendipity when Second World War enemy action blew out the Victorian stained glass windows which were then replaced with the plain glass making the church brighter and lighter.

Paddle Steamer *Waverley* at Southwold Pier

Waverley is the last sea-going paddle steamer in the world and is included in the Historic Ships Register. Built in 1946 to replace the original *Waverley* which sank during minesweeping duties at Dunkirk in 1940, the steamer worked originally on the River Clyde. Here she is at the restored Southwold Pier, at the start of a day trip to the River Thames and Tower Bridge. The inland stretch of water is a boating lake, part of Buss Creek (a Buss was a type of Dutch fishing boat) which meets with the River Blyth west of the town.

Easton Bavents

This is one of the most eroded parts of the Suffolk coast. Easton Ness and the village of Easton Stone were washed into the sea centuries ago as was Easton Bavents church around 1700. Half of the village has been washed away since 1939 and the future of the remaining properties looks bleak.

Opposite: **Easton Bavents looking north**

Retired engineer Peter Boggis has been fighting to save the remaining thirteen properties in Easton Bavents, at no cost to the taxpayer, by importing thousands of tons of clay soil which is placed at the base of the cliffs. This soil is 'sacrificed' (washed away) instead of this happening to the cliffs behind the imported soil. And there's a secondary benefit because, as it erodes, the imported soil helps build up the beaches southwards in the movement of sedimentary longshore drift. In a battle first with the local council regarding planning permissions and subsequently with Natural England (the former Nature Conservancy a couple of name changes ago) the problem has now reached the High Court. Natural England wants the sea to take its course thereby revealing fossils and rocks for geological study. Mr Boggis wants the right to prevent properties falling down the cliff.

Further north is the breached Easton Broad with Covehithe Broad and Benacre Broad in the distance.

Easton Bavents October 1999
The yellow line marks cliff erosion at October 2008.

October 2008

'Thurlesley' on the cliffs at Easton Bavents. Part of the sacrificial sea defence can still be seen in the left foreground. This gave the house an additional eight years of survival. It is unlikely to survive another fierce storm.

Easton Broad & Reedbeds

Suffolk Wildlife Trust has created several new reedbeds in the area including here at Easton Broad for over-wintering birds, as a landfall for migratory birds, and as a refuge for mammals. But the problem of sea incursion is expected to reduce reedbed areas within the next 30-100 years. Easton and Covehithe Broads probably are the remains of a Viking estuary.

Covehithe Broad

Covehithe, Easton and Benacre Broads have at least two things in common. They all have NNR (National Nature Reserve) status and they're both diminishing as the sea erodes them.

Covehithe - the end of the road

Covehithe was once a small fishing port and this road led down to the beach where fishing boats were pulled up onto the sand and shingle. The sea swallowed the port and continues to swallow the road year by year. St Andrew's church is, like Walberswick's, a church within a church. Cromwell's men ruined the original during the Civil War so a smaller church was built Russian-doll-style inside the shell.

Benacre Broad looking towards Lowestoft

Benacre breached
Salt water incursion has killed certain tree species.

Inspecting the breach

Benacre looking south, with Southwold in the distance
The existences of Benacre Broad and Covehithe Broad seem unlikely to remain for much longer if present conditions continue.

Benacre pits looking north towards Lowestoft

The pits were caused by shingle excavation for airfield construction during the Second World War.

Benacre Sluice

The outlet of the Hundred River is now below sea level and water has to be pumped up on to the beach.

Kessingland looking east

Wisely, in view of the fate of coastal churches further south, the fifteenth century church was built well inland, with the tower serving as a beacon for shipping. Modern houses dominate today with most of their occupants having jobs outside the village. But during the reign of William the Conqueror, Kessingland was the most important haven between Great Yarmouth and Dunwich and one of the richest places on the Suffolk coast.

Kessingland looking east

Here's the answer provided by Peter Boggis of Easton Bavents who knows a thing or two about beach erosion:

To understand why the beach at Kessingland is building when so many nearby are eroding it's necessary to go back several centuries. Four hundred years ago Easton Ness (now washed away) projected nearly two miles out to sea and was the most easterly point in Britain. Either side of the Ness were high cliffs surrounded by peat beds and shingle beaches. To serve a growing population with fuel the peat was dug out, man transported it along local rivers by keel, subsequently by wherry. Peat extraction exposed the Ness to erosion and was one of the major factors contributing to the demise of Dunwich because the Ness had previously protected the port from the ravages of northerly winds. With Easton Ness gone, beach material moved northwards to Benacre thereby closing the mouth of the Hundred River around 1715. This allowed Benacre Ness to build as it moved slowly northwards. The Ness was fed by sediments from eroding cliffs and more importantly by material from the Barnard Sands one mile offshore. The material was carried in and out by wind and tide. In the 1970s there was extensive offshore dredging south of the Barnard Sands and this halted the feeder sediment flow to the coast which in turn resulted in a sharp increase in erosion south of the Ness. A new groyne system was built at Kessingland in 1975/6 which stopped longshore drift movement of material to and from Benacre Ness. A new Ness at Kessingland beach began to build rapidly filling the groyne system and this in itself has stopped the drift of materials southwards thereby causing even greater erosion to the south.

Pakefield Coastwatch

Coastwatch is a voluntary organisation assisting HM Coastguard. This lighthouse now used by Coastwatch was first lit in 1832 to warn shipping about inshore sandbanks. In the 1930s the holiday camp which now surrounds it was opened. During the Second World War it was taken over by the Royal Observer Corps and in 2000 it was renovated as a Coastal Surveillance (i.e. Coastwatch) station.

Huts, boats and beach

Since there is no natural harbour, fishing boats are pulled up onto the beach. Rod and line fishing from the beach is common.

Pakefield

Pakefield, together with most of the seaside villages of Norfolk and Suffolk, had a thriving Beach Company (forerunners of the lifeboat service). Saving lives and salvaging vessels were their stated aims and whether they were always honest or not their courage in launching into turbulent seas for rescues is undisputed.

Was the crock of gold found in Pakefield or in Lowestoft?

Pakefield and Lowestoft
From this picture it's easy to see how a gap driven through the beach created a harbour.

Brooke Marine

Sadly no more, but the Brooke yards provided employment for boat builders and repairers for over a hundred years. The yard closed in 1992 but in this picture there are hopeful signs that a smaller enterprise is starting up.

Opposite: **Lowestoft harbour entrance**

Entrepreneur Samuel Morton Peto, a Victorian of tremendous vision and energy, saw the benefits to be gained from a flourishing port to rival Great Yarmouth. In 1847 he expanded the harbour again to create entrance piers, with a light on the south pier to guide ships through the narrow gap. To the right is the Trawl Dock where the fishing fleet used to moor (when there was a fishing fleet). To the left is the marina of the Royal Norfolk and Suffolk Yacht Club. The Inner Harbour starts on the far side of the bascule bridge and encompasses Lake Lothing.

Mutford Lock and Oulton Broad

The creation of Mutford Lock, to provide access to the River Yare via the Broads network and so on to Norwich, was part of the grand scheme to open up Lowestoft as a port. The aim was to provide ships with access to Norwich without going through Great Yarmouth with its high tolls and silted harbour. How different this scene would have been if the enterprise had been commercially successful. Because it has to cope with tides coming both from Lowestoft and three hours later from the Great Yarmouth direction via the River Waveney the lock has sea gates at either end. To cope with tall masts the railway swing bridge near the lock opens in conjunction with the lock. Oulton Broad is at the southernmost end of the Broads and today only pleasure craft use its waters.

Opposite: **Oulton Broad and Lowestoft**

On the skyline is a single wind turbine nicknamed 'Gulliver'. It dominates the whole town. Oulton Broad has pretty houses with water frontages; foreground right are Suffolk Wildlife Trust's Carlton Marshes.

Lake Lothing
The tidal lake links to Lowestoft's Inner harbour. Near the harbour piers (left of picture) are the Waveney and Hamilton Docks..

Steamship *Robin*

Built 1890 at Bow Creek in London, *Robin* spent most of her working life in Spanish, French and English coastal waters. Her commercial working life ended in 1974 when she was bought by The Maritime Trust subsequently taken over by the *Robin* Trust. She's currently at Small & Co's yard in the Inner Harbour for refurbishment.

Lowestoft landmarks

In 1609 Trinity House received a petition from merchants and shipowners to build two lighthouses at Lowestoft *"for the direction of ships which crept in by night in the dangerous passage betwixt Lowestoft and Winterton"*. The lights enabled ships to line up on them for guidance through the Stamford Channel and clear of the sandbanks. The Low Light was victim of sea erosion but the High Light remains working.

In Belle View Park stands a poignant War Memorial erected and maintained by the War Graves Commission and dedicated to the memory of *"those who have no known grave but the sea"*. Many of the 2,385 names engraved were men of the Royal Naval Patrol Service and an high percentage of Lowestoft trawlermen were among their number. Mike Page's father was a trawler skipper in the RNVR and he died at sea in 1942 but is buried elsewhere.

The large house down the slope was Robert Sparrow's holiday house bought by Lowestoft Corporation for the benefit of the town to celebrate Queen Victoria's Diamond Jubilee 1897. It stands in the aptly named 'Sparrows Nest Park'. The house contains the RN Patrol Service Museum but during the Second World War it became HMS *Europa*.

Lowestoft to Great Yarmouth

Ness Point is the most easterly piece of land in Britain but it's commemorated merely by a circle in the promenade floor and called the Euroscope - it gives distances to other places in Europe. All in all the site is fairly unremarkable but there's a growing body of opinion urging a more significant commemoration. Nearby, the Beach Village, home of the fishing community, was demolished in the 1960s partly because it was prone to flooding and partly in a slum clearance scheme. Short-sightedly not one cottage was left standing and, even worse, this prime site was sold for industrial development. What a wasted opportunity!

The first green area along the front was where the fishing nets used to be hung to dry and waited for the attention of the beatsters, usually female, who mended the nets.

Corton

Once a Roman signal station, then a landmark for shipping and a Victorian resort with fine houses along the cliff, then a nudist beach which closed recently because of coastal erosion, now best known for its theme park New Pleasurewood Hills - Suffolk's answer to Alton Towers.

Wipeout in winter

'Wipeout' - an inverting roller coaster - is the latest attraction at New Pleasurewood Hills. The park first opened in 1980 and has added new rides each year.

Hopton homes and holidays
Permanent residents and holiday makers are about equal in number in Hopton.

Opposite: **Hopton holidays**
The ever popular caravan holiday. The beach revetments have been effective in preventing cliff erosion.

Hopton looking north towards Gorleston and Great Yarmouth

The county boundary changed resulting in Hopton moving from Norfolk to Suffolk. Gorleston Golf Club, the first of many Norfolk Golf Clubs at the sea's edge, separates Hopton from Gorleston northwards. Gorleston Pier has provided a barrier to longshore drift recently causing loss of sand from Gorleston beach. The effect of Great Yarmouth's new Outer Harbour on longshore drift to the south is also unknown. Breydon Water is in the distance, it flows into the River Yare which in turn flows between Yarmouth's North and South Quays and out to sea at Gorleston Pier.